For Gladys O'connel
none of this would h

Adapted by Sharon O'connell (AKA Number One)
from the diary of Jerry O'connell

Prologue

Someone said, "Jerry, you should write all this down." So I did.

Chapter 1 New beginnings

Being self-employed in the building industry in the 80's was not the easiest of times to make money. The Thatcher years brought financial hardship to thousands upon thousands of striking miners and public sector workers. And builders. Money was tight for everyone, and everyone was tight in Yorkshire. No one had the finances to build extensions, convert their attics or repair rooves. Inevitably this didn't deter folk from having this work done - they just didn't have the means of paying for it. This left me severely out of pocket and facing crippling debts. When I raised my pint of bitter in the Royal Standard in 1979 and pledged to 'Be my own boss,' I had no inkling that I would have to endure a decade of sleepless nights, working through sickness in all weathers, and wondering if I had earnt enough to cover my weekly rent to the Council.

By 1989 I'd had enough. I landed my first salaried job since I left the building firm where I had completed my apprenticeship. And it was shit. Pig shit. Tonnes of the stuff that I spent my days shovelling. Not quite on a par with converting a millionaire's farmhouse near Sowerby Bridge {a job I actually did get paid well for} but it had two advantages. Firstly, I knew that I would have the comforting feeling of an envelope full of notes in my back pocket every Friday. Even better, who would have dreamt that the stench of ammonia emanating from the muck reminded me of the smell of my B&H fags. I stopped smoking immediately and have never so much as craved a cigarette since.

It was while I was travelling to the pig farm one misty, dank morning that I drove past a For Sale board attached to the side of a white painted cottage in the middle of nowhere. I didn't think any more about the place, my mind was full of worry about paying the bank loan off and the soaring interest rates.

A few weeks later after a particularly wet and windy weekend in Beverley, I was driving to work on Monday morning and noticed the For Sale sign again. I slowed down this time and saw that the cottage was infact a village Post Office with living space attached. I could suddenly imagine me, my wife and our children, escaping the life of hustle and bustle of a busy Yorkshire market town and running a thriving village business in the heart of God's own county. I may have spent the rest of the day shovelling you know what, but my head was swirling with ideas about how I could turn the rundown village Post Office into a thriving emporium.

They say history repeats itself. Here I was again, ready to be my own boss, and I didn't have a clue what I was letting myself in for.

Chapter 2 Escape to the country

One financially crippling bridging loan later, we made the twenty mile move north, to the small village of Tibthorpe in East Yorkshire. The Post Office and shop were situated to the side of the B1248 - a busyish road leading to the North Yorkshire Moors and a popular route for bikers and cyclists. The building consisted of a medium sized shop with a few dusty shelves and an attached Post Office counter with an old-fashioned glass front. A dark and narrow passageway lead to a small sitting room, a rundown kitchen and upstairs, three small bedrooms. It was cold, dusty, and unloved. Like Miss Haversham's front room but missing the moth-eaten wedding cake.

I was thinking big; Barbour jackets, shooting accessories, Hunters wellingtons. I imagined a packed retail hub heaving with local gentry and ruddy cheeked farmers' wives carrying gingham baskets brimming with our locally sourced produce. In my head, we would easily pay off our bridging loan and the hefty mortgage on our new country pile.

Both naturally early risers, my wife Christine and I were undaunted by the daily 6am alarm, opening the shop before most people were even awake, to receive deliveries of daily provisions and newspapers. With no previous retail experience, we threw ourselves into navigating around a whole new way of life. Inevitably we made many mistakes on the way, nevertheless, over the next decade, we managed to scratch an existence from selling comestibles -and even occasionally Barbour jackets- to the local villagers and day trippers bound for the delights of the North Yorkshire Moors.

The working day in the shop passed slowly. It was bitterly cold in the winter months and whilst trade was steady throughout the day, we were never rushed off our feet. We soon realised that this venture was never going to be an escape route out of growing debt. However slowly but surely, we began to get to know the regulars to Tibthorpe Stores. Not unlike anyone who works in a rural hub, we soon began to delight in the daily conversations and events shared by our customers. Yes, our feet were like blocks of ice in our slippers, but these interactions warmed our hearts and occasionally made us feel like moving to the countryside to run a village shop had been a good decision after all.

Chapter 3 The first customers

I remember my debut as a retail entrepreneur as if it was yesterday. Our very first customer, an elderly gentleman who introduced himself as 'Dave' walked through the door and was obviously a local man as he did not pull up in a car. Without looking up from the floor he whispered, "Please can I have a pint of…." At this point, eager to clinch my first sale with efficiency and style, I reached out into the fridge and asked him if he'd prefer semi skimmed or whole milk. He lifted his gaze and his eyes met mine, bewildered and wide. "Please can I have a pint of paraffin," his sentence now completed, he seemed fearful of what I would offer him next. I told him that if he was planning to keep warm, a pint wouldn't last him long. Being a rural store, paraffin actually was in stock, and as I handed him the bottle, he took it from me like it contained the elixir of eternal youth. He then informed me that he would be spending that afternoon "cleaning things down." My mind boggled.

My second customer was a mother accompanied by two young children who proceeded to run around the shop screaming like banshees and throwing handfuls of sweets taken from the shelf at each other; she appeared blissfully unaware and selectively short of hearing. One of the delightful goblins walked over to me and shouted, "Who are you?" I replied, "I'm Father Christmas and you will be getting nowt for Christmas this year." After drawing breath, her firstborn dropped onto his knees and let out a hysterical cry followed by several loud sobs. The once passive and complacent mother scooped up both of her offspring and asked me how dare I treat my customers like that. As I watched her leave, slamming the door behind her, and almost knocking the hinged door bell off its bracket, I wondered what living hell I would have to deal with next. It must have taken me five solid minutes to pick up the Twix's and Mars bars off the shop floor.

Chapter 4 Brace yourselves

Back in the early 90's – in the days where branch Post Offices were still a thing and people used actual money – the village of approximately 157 inhabitants had a Policewoman in its ranks. One of my earliest memories of working in the shop was hearing the loud crash of metal on metal; the ear-splitting sound coming from the road at the side of the shop. It transpired that a gentleman from Driffield had been a little too eager in overtaking a tractor on the country road and had been forced to swerve to the left to avoid an oncoming car. In doing so, he drove into the back of a car parked opposite our shop. Not just any car unfortunately. It belonged to our very own Juliet Bravo. Fortunately, no one was in her car and the damage sustained was minor; a broken brake light and a small dint in the bumper. Not so great was the state of the written off car of Mr Driffield, although thankfully, he was uninjured. We took him in, offered him a cup of tea with sugar 'for the shock,' and let him ring his wife on our landline (no mobile phones in those days) so she could collect him. Later that day we saw a woman walking stiffly towards the shop clutching at a neck brace that was clearly causing her some discomfort. It was Claire – the village bobby. I was clearly confused as I knew she wasn't in her car when it was hit by the driver earlier that morning. Before I had chance to speak, she muttered, "I'm going to need time off work because of this bloody accident. I'm in agony with my neck."

I remained clueless as to how a women could have sustained such a painful and work threatening injury without being anywhere near her car, until I summoned up the courage to ask her that very question. She replied, "I was in my bathroom cleaning my teeth when I heard him crash into my car and the shock caused my neck to crick." Surely the first and last time the act of dental brushing has resulted in the wearing of a neck brace.

Chapter 5 Mr Dick

Whilst my customers not paying me for goods and services was a huge problem back in my days as a self-employed builder, luckily this abhorrent trait didn't follow me into my new business like a financial grim reaper anywhere near as much as it used to. However - there were still close shaves.

Only a few months into the business, I was loading a box of groceries into the boot of a car for an elderly local woman, when I heard a grunting sound. I began to investigate; the noise appeared to be coming from underneath the vehicle. I peered into the front grid and saw a dog's face looking at me helplessly. It seemed that her pet canine – called Mr Dick (don't ask) – had somehow become trapped. His owner appeared to be unsurprised by this scenario and said, "He's blind and almost dead, you know." I stood there and remember thinking, 'I hope Mr Dick doesn't drop off the hook soon, as the old bat hasn't paid me yet for the three cases of dog food I've just loaded into her boot'.

Chapter 6 Fond memories

Don't get me wrong. There were many advantages to living in the countryside despite having no money. Taking my black Labrador, Sam, out for dawn walks in Low Wood and marvelling at pheasants springing out from their leafy hiding places as we strolled past them gave me a feeling of calm and justification that we had done the right thing after all. I remember one particularly crisp morning where I took the time to sit down on a fallen tree and take in the scenery. Sam was delighted with his new country home and confirmed this by sticking his snout deep into a rabbit hole after picking up animal scent. What more could a shopkeeper ask for!

We used to open the shop a little later at 9am on Sundays. Sundays were my favourite day of the week – always five or so minutes between customers – just the job!

Chapter 7 Community Service

We quickly realised that we weren't just serving the village with food, drink, and other essential items. Only a few months into the job, the locals began leaving us the spare keys to their houses with the assumed premise that we'd be happy to help them out if they lost or misplaced their keys, or had a visitor to stay who may need a spare set. And the expectation that this community service that they had forced upon us without question, also involved any one of them knocking on our door out of hours - and I mean in the very late and early hours - to ask for their key as if they were doing us a favour. This included the local Police Officer....

As there were no gas pipe mains to the village, another community service role was ensuring we were stocked up with enough calor gas bottles to meet the constant demand. My heart always sank when the bottles were delivered to the front of the store. Not only were the cylinders heavy, but I would regularly lose at least two miles of skin from each ankle lifting them to the back of the shop.

The colder and more inclement the weather, the better, as far as we were concerned. One particularly chilly winter morning, the snow began to fall from the sky in fist sized flakes and coated the road outside in seconds. "That'll stop the buggers going into town to buy their shopping today," Christine announced with utter joy and a gleam of pound signs in her eyes.

Christine always let me know how busy the store had been whenever I was working elsewhere. I always dreaded the words, "Today was a slow day," as I inevitably knew that meant we were one day even further away from our dream retirement. After one such day, we opened our 'Customer slate' book. Looking at the outstanding debts, we agreed that half of the villagers would have died of starvation without our willingness to give them credit. Nevertheless, in the five years we had run the shop at this point, we, always received our back payments eventually. We never put pressure on anyone to pay up their debts, and our rule of, 'pay even a little when you can,' served us and the villagers well. That's definitely one in the eye for supermarket chains – 'No money Sir? – Well put the bugger back on the shelf then.'

Saying that, if any of our customers hadn't paid up, I'd have put a bloody sign up with their name on in the shop window….and they knew it!

We were persuaded to join the village committee given our key role as the village hub. We imagined this would be forum for planning exciting summer fetes and debaucherous cheese and wine evenings. The reality was seven of us shivering in an unheated village hall for two hours once a year with nothing of note on the agenda, whilst the remaining 137 inhabitants of the village were no doubt stuffing their faces with Port Salut washed down with vintage Dom Perignon warm and onesie clad at home.

A dentist moved into one of the village houses and asked us if we could help him to set up some post office savings accounts. I let slip that there was a beautiful woodland area where I walked Sam every morning at 6.30am. An hour later he rang me to ask if he could join me on my 6.30am walk on Sunday morning. You see, as well being a shopkeeper and the local builder, I'm apparently also the village gamekeeper. He did turn up to join me, for the record. During the walk he talked about how difficult his job could be at times. I said, "Well at least your bloody customers can't complain with their mouths wide open."

Christine became very adept at providing a counselling service for couples who were having relationship issues. People would go into minute details about their other half and their numerous shortcomings, and often in graphic detail. Others were just not happy with their lot. One customer, Alice, confided that she'd filed for a divorce because her husband was 'too old fashioned' – despite him paying for their children to receive a private education and for them all to drive round in prestige cars. My take on this is that nobody gets exactly what they want out of life, so why can't we just settle for second best and be happy with what we've got?

Turned out that everyone in the village knew the intricate details of Alice's divorce. Some sources initially reported that she had a 'toy boy' on the go, but as the rumour mill gained momentum, all manner of sexual deviances were attached to her private life.

Yet another request from community members was to use our loo if they were caught short whilst shopping. Norris Jones, a senior gentleman, asked me if he could use the toilet one day which was, of course, fine by me. As quick as a flash, Helena, another of our regulars said, "Norris, can I come in the toilet with you and hold it for you?" "Yes, but only if you put your false teeth back in," was his drole response.

Chapter 8 – RUDE CUSTOMERS

One customer who we nicknamed 'Big M' from a neighbouring village was a particularly churlish character. Whenever my wife noticed her walking into the shop, she used to hide under the counter and hope that Big M would leave the premises out of frustration that no one was there to serve her.

On another occasion, on our one day off per week, I took Christine to the hairdressers, and she decided to have her hair cut very short. The next day, my wife told me that every single customer, without fail, had asked her if she'd had her hair cut. Some might say that it was flattering of them all to take notice and make a comment about it. I might say that there was sod all else to talk about in the village, so a simple, everyday occurrence opened up a whole can of bored worms. Later the same day, when I joined Christine in the shop, a deaf gentleman I mentioned earlier entered the shop and also asked my now raging other half if she'd had her hair cut. Instead of her politely replying with her previous response on repeat, she snapped, "No. It's a swimming cap." In an attempt to make light of this situation which was souring rapidly, I defaulted to my 'Carry On' humour and told him it was, "a Dutch cap."

"It's not, is it?" retorted our hearing aid clad customer. "Never seen one of them before now, " before exiting the store with a bemused look on his face.

Chapter 9 The Village Jokers

Every village has its fair share of characters and ours was certainly not an exception to the rule. Not long after we opened the shop, whilst carrying a box of groceries to a customer's car, I noticed a new addition to our village notices and adverts board. A mystery resident had cut out pictures of a prominent couple, our village's very own Posh and Becks, and carefully added glasses, beards, and smoking pipes to their previously beaming faces. I raced back into the shop and yelled out to Christine that there was something she needed to see. She rushed outside and ripped the masterpiece from the notice board. "If she sees that, she will do her nut", hissed my panicked wife. Needless to say, we never did discover who the was responsible for the village Banksy.

Chapter 10 The Slug

I didn't turn my back entirely on the building trade
and continued to take on construction work for local
people and friends. The work began to come in thick

and fast and I thought it wise to hire a labourer to assist me in my endeavours.

On one particularly cold and frosty morning having returned from the warehouse run, I had a job lined up to build a garden wall for a local man. However, before I could commence this side hustle, my day began with a drive to the warehouse, some 30 miles away, at 6.30am – the one time of the day that we could rest easy, knowing that the shoplifters wouldn't be up and about yet.

On returning home, I dropped the stock off and headed over to the building job. 'The Slug' aka my labourer. and named thus as he only had two speeds, 'Slow' and 'Stop,' was late again.

After I'd finished work for the day, my head addled after with a day of working alongside The Slug, I headed home and bumped into another shop regular who was not sporting his hearing aids as he usually did. If only for my own non PC amusement, I began a lengthy and silent monologue about the day I'd had, opening and closing my mouth like a fish. "Daft sod, " he chuckled as he eventually realised what I was doing.

Our next exchange was equally amusing. We had a battery powered alarm in the shop which began to buzz loudly as the battery ran down. Customer after customer came into the shop and would ask us what the buzzing noise was. My standard reply was, "What bloody buzzing? I can't hear a thing."

After a few days of gaslighting everyone into believing they were hearing things, this audio challenged gentleman came into the shop and asked me the very same question. Once again I denied all knowledge of what the noise was, which in reality, was becoming increasingly loud and annoying. I asked him if I could borrow his hearing aids." Barmy bugger," he replied, knowing once again that he'd been a victim of my schoolboy humour.

The Slug, by name and nature, was late, yet again, for our next job. No doubt pootling along at 20 miles an hour in his Fiat 500 or more aptly dubbed the 'Slug mobile.' When he eventually appeared (extracting himself from his Italian sardine can at a similar speed to a sloth climbing up into a vertical jungle canopy wearing a rucksack full of lead), he declared, "I'm hungry." "I'm hungry."

The Slug always says everything twice because he is so boring that no one ever listens to him when he says things the first time.

On another occasion, he turned up almost an hour and a half late to another building job that I had lined him up to labour for me. His excuse this time was, "I couldn't get past a lorry." As far as I'm concerned, the Slug couldn't get past a one-legged cat.

Only once can I remember the slug being 'early.' On this sacred and unprecedented day, he declared that he and his wife had had 'words over money' and he was adamant that he wanted a 'flat of his own'. He delivered this prophetic statement as if he had finally seen the light after years lost in a darkened wilderness. The thing was that I had heard this proclamation a hundred times before. Needless to say, for our next job, he was late again.

And for the next. It was a beautiful, sunshiny bright morning- the first day of Spring if I remember correctly. By lunchtime, the sun was flexing its solar muscles at long last after a cold and endless winter. I took my jumper off and enjoyed the feeling of warmth on my bare arms (It's never too early to start your annual builder's tan). I made the mistake of asking the Slug if he was going to take his thick overcoat off to enjoy the ambient temperature. I was met with, "Ne'er cast a clout till May is out." (Repeated, inevitably).

The fact is that the Slug keeps his overcoat, jumper and heavy work trousers on all year round – even in the middle of summer. I made the foolish mistake of asking the slug if he was sweating with all of these clothes on. "No, I don't," he explained. "I wear Tupperware underpants – they keep everything you've got fresh."

Do I have to tell you again that he was late for work another morning? Surely not. Well, he was, and his excuse this time, "I've been thinking a lot." I could only imagine where his Socratic thought process had taken him. "My ex-wife has sold our house and I'm going to get £10,000. My share of the house and my divorce will come through at the same time."

"So, you're old, free and single," I stated. The slug made a sound like a cat caught under a tractor wheel. "Yes, I'm old, free and single. Yes, I'm old, free and single."

Late. Again. When he eventually appeared, he let out a series of monumental farts and then continued to break wind throughout the day. I suggested he go to the Doctor's to get some powders. He replied, "My new girlfriend doesn't let me fart in the house, so I have to save it up and let it go when I come to work."

"Come to work a bloody hour later then and get rid of it all before you start work then," was my response. "Nowt wrong with a bit of wind. " "Nowt wrong with a bit of wind."

And yet again. *Two* hours late this time. The reason on this occasion was, "I was late because I can't stop thinking about my birthday." Words failed me. Funnily enough, the slug splashed out on a holiday on one of the Costas for himself and his new love interest. Were they late for the flight? Were they buggery.

But, of course, he was late for work the first day he returned from his holiday. "Because whenever you come back from a holiday, it makes you tired," was this morning's justification for his tardiness. The day after, it was "It was head wind, and the car doesn't like head wind."

"Well one day you might have a back wind and you'll be early?" I queried. "I'd have to be putting my foot on the brake. Car doesn't like going over 40 miles an hour."

What can a man reply to that logic? He's a bloody nutter.

Chapter 11 – The golden rules

The Saturday morning rush saw our customers come in in their droves to buy their papers, fags and milk. We also became quickly accustomed to those who clearly had zero intention of parting with their cash, but just walked in because they fancied a chat and catch up on the village gossip, which would invariably last for twenty minutes plus of keeping us talking when we had other paying customers waiting.

We soon became wise to these pleasant timewasters, and one Bushmills fuelled evening, we devised a golden rule which displayed business acumen that even Lord Sugar would be proud of.

Our mantra became, 'If they spend more than £30 that week in the shop, we will happily spend the time of day filling them in on the latest goings on in the village. Any amount less, and then *they* must tell *us* the gossip.

Let's face it. In a village where there is nothing else going on, and I mean, nothing – we get to know EVERYTHING!!

As a Virgo, I am meticulously tidy – some may call it OCD, in my desire to have everything in its place. Every morning I would spend a considerable amount of time before we opened, tidying the shelves and putting any misplaced stock into their correct positions. My wife, on the other hand, does not share the same astrological traits as me. This caused us both an untold amount of stress; however, our golden rule was to NEVER argue in front of customers.

Chapter 12 Chap

At the end of one particularly arduous Saturday, we finally managed to sit down in front of a roaring log fire. As I was about to take my first sip of a well-deserved glass of wine, the telephone rang.

"Now then chap. I'm pissed as a rat, "declared the mournful voice from the handset. I instantly recognised the dulcet tones of Tim, a super hardworking farm labourer, and a regular visitor to our shop. He only drank on Saturdays, starting at 10am and not stopping until he could no longer stand up unaided.

"Will you ring our Deirdre for me and tell her that I love her?" he slurred. "If I ring her, she'll tell me off for being pissed again."

I told Tim that I would happily call Deirdre for him to pass on this heart-warming message and asked for her number. He then proceeded to call out a series of random numbers which reminded me of a dyscalculic bingo caller at the Regal in Beverley. After numerous attempts, he managed to string a series of digits together which were bordering on coherent. I repeated them back to him and he confidently replied, "That's the one chap." (Tim only ever called anyone and everyone 'Chap' when he was pissed).

In my unenviable and unsought role as community service worker, I promptly called Deirdre, Tim's sister, to inform her that Tim 'loved her.' In true Hilda Ogden mode I knew she was pursing her pursing her lips as she snapped back, "Oh so he's pissed again is he? Tell him to go to bed and sleep it off."

Having completed my community service for the evening, I finally felt that I could relax back into my armchair and breathe a sigh of relief that I had done the right thing.

More fool me...The telephone rang an hour later. "Hello chap. Can I come to the shop now to pay my bill? I can't pay it in the morning, because I'll be too tired." Unsure of which path this alcohol fuelled train of thought was leading us down, I asked Tim why he would be too tired.

"Because I'll be up all night worrying about me not paying the bill, Chap."

The community officer in me kicked straight in and I told him to knock on our door and he could settle up with us. "Thanks chap, "he gushed. "I think you're the best and I love you Chap."

True to his word, not more than thirty minutes later I heard a knock at the door. He paid us the money he owed and purchased some bacon and eggs for his breakfast, before wobbling his way back towards his house.

This very same gentleman came into the shop one afternoon in Spring and declared to Christine that he had some bad news. He informed my wife that a young lad who worked at a nearby farm, and who we knew as a regular customer, had died of brain cancer. Such sad news affected us all and we continued the day in a sombre and reflective state, thinking how short life is and how we must make the best of it.

Less than twenty-four hours later, the very same young lad, whose passing we were currently mourning, more vibrant and alive than I had seen anyone in my whole life, strode into the shop and asked for a packet of Marlborough. Christine did a double take to check that this was not a ghostly visitation. Turns out that Chap got the wrong end of the stick again.

During a very busy Saturday morning when the customers were really flashing the cash, Chap came scuttling in with his head down. "What's wrong Tim?" I enquired. With a shake of his weary head, he replied, I went out last night instead of all day Saturday and got really pissed. You see – Friday night's not as long as all day Saturday. Anyway, I got home at 1.30 am and I couldn't find my bloody door key. Next thing I know, it's Saturday morning and my bloody dog is licking me ear Chap and I'm curled up in the dog bed."

Tim purchased his hangover staple of bacon and eggs and declared to anyone who was listening, "I'm as stiff as a fart."

Chapter 12 "I'm a size 4 but a 12 feels so good".

We called her Olive Oil given her languid, flailing limbs which windmilled around the shop, gesticulating at the items she wanted. Her expectation was that we would effectively run around the shop for her as, God forbid, she might have to pick up a tin for herself.

Given that warehouse visits always consisted of me, sweating, and struggling to drag a heavy trolley around whilst Christine simply pointed to what she wanted me to add to the load, I reckoned that perhaps she had learnt too much from our village Olive).

Thanks to our £30 plus customers, we were dutifully informed that Olive's father had recently passed, leaving her a hefty inheritance, and that she'd judiciously placed this into a TESSA. However. Olive persisted in informing us that she was struggling financially, whilst displaying perpetual illusions of grandeur.

For once and once only, the slug got it right. "She wouldn't give you the smell off her fart." Tibthorpe's very own poet laureate had spoken.

Chapter 13 Sugar

We both had to go to the dentist after years of no treatment needed. The fillings we now required appeared to be inversely proportional to the amount of pick and mix we were both snacking on as a result of working in the shop.

A later trip to the dentist was equally alarming. No fillings this time - but when we parked up, we spotted two skinheads selling small packets with white powder in them from the window of a black sports car to hapless teenagers. Never before had I observed such a waste of human life – people selling death in a little plastic bag. But what will happen when the Police catch them? Nowt. Pushers and users are no good to anyone in this world. I would give them all a year's supply, all at once as a punishment and force them to take it.

To fight the flab gained through our diabetes inducing diet, Christine decided to join the village aerobics class which used to take place weekly in the village hall. I walked to meet her one evening after her class, but as an infamously - early for everything- man, I looked through the window and was faced with the startling view of forty fat bums jiggling from left to right. That was the last time I met her from aerobics. Still – whatever makes her happy.

Chapter 14 Pension Day

Village folk are creatures of habit, and none more so than its silver surfers (although that phrase hadn't been invented in the 90's). You could set your clock by the local elders calling into the Post Office section of the shop to collect their pension.

The first through the door, moving at a pace that would leave Usain Bolt in the starting blocks, would be Reg. He perpetually wore a face that could turn even highly sterilised milk sour, expect for the second when he had his handout in his mitts, whereupon a dashing beam of his smile would instantaneously light up even the darkest recesses of the shop. "Have you heard about Earnest?" said Reg as he immediately switched back to his gloomy self. (Earnest has the coveted title of being Reg's neighbour). "He waited in all morning for his new telly to be delivered but they didn't turn up…. So, Earnest nipped outside for a quick word with a woman over the fence." He paused for dramatic effect, then continued, "I heard the TV man knocking on his door, but he buggered off when no-one answered. It's his own fault. He should have been in." The milk of human kindness runs very thin at times in the village.

Chapter 15 – Domestic Bliss

One of the less optimistic records of our daily life reads, and I quote, "What a crap day. Not busy at all. This makes Christine stomp about all day with a face like a bulldog chewing a wasp. Then I get it in the neck with comments like, 'It's your fault there are no customers today – you are always cheeky to them.' 'Things are too expensive,'- 'Do you think the shop needs refitting again? – 'Let's have a sale.' The moral of this story is that you can never win with a woman who runs a shop.

Another golden moment in the history of our relationship took place after I'd   spent hours completing some particularly labour intensive modernisation work in our kitchen. This resulted in large quantities of dust dispersing and settling throughout our house and the shop. As I headed upstairs to take a much-needed shower, I heard Christine serving a customer. When asked the price of a particular good, she replied, "39p and the dust is free."

I wear my heart on my sleeve and how I feel is etched all over my face. Its genetic – my mother and father were exactly the same. However, my wife is from a far- flung genetic pool (Hammond Road), where she is able to raise a smile for even the most rancid of customers. God help me though, when the door closed and she was in one of her legendary moods…. And then the sudden 'ping' of the glorious shop bell would ring out again, and my very own Stepford wife would re-emerge into our retail emporium to serve the customer with a smile worthy of the King of England.

I live according to the mantra, 'It's a woman's prerogative to change her mind.' This was especially true on filling up the van with supplies from the warehouse every week. Without fail, Christine would deliver the same phrase. "I've spent too much again." Shortly afterwards, this would be followed by a monologue in which she would justify to herself why she hadn't spent too much.

One particularly cold morning, I opened the shop at 8.30am (normally Christine's job) and shouted upstairs to inform her that she was late. She shouted, "I'm just putting my face on, "to which I (predictably) replied, "Shall I bring you a shovel?"

For those of you with a half decent memory, you will remember me talking about my dark days of shovelling pig shit to make ends meet ('meat', as

Richard Whiteley, the countdown King of Wetwang, would inevitably have punned had he adapted these memoires). Anyway, I was called back to the pig farm with the brief of building something which would 'stop the pigs crapping in their food.' Having designed, then created, a feat of modern engineering which would have the Dragon's Den judges pistol dualling to have the right to buy, I strode like ten men, back into the shop. I was bursting with pride, and eager to tell Christine all about my genius innovation. "Get straight in the shower Jerry. You stink of pig shit."

.

Chapter 16 – No smoke without fire

We'd had a beautiful drive to the warehouse that morning and witnessed one of those sunrises that will stay in your mind forever. On returning to the shop, I set off to another building job directly opposite the shop, and waited to be joined by my labourer, the Slug, who in a surprise turn of events, was late again. Still energised by dawn's delight, I heard Christine screaming," Jerry, Jerry." "Come to the shop, it's on fire." I didn't rush to get back. To be honest I was hoping that the whole bloody lot would be burnt to a crisp by the time I got there. Going through the doorway, my nostrils were indeed filled with a smell of burning, and I followed my nose to the main display fridge. It was clear to me that the motor had burnt out after years of hard labour.

Christine rang our local electrician and explained the situation. He informed us that he didn't have a motor available but would come back tomorrow and fix it.

Expecting nothing less, every single customer that day who subsequently entered the store took a good old sniff and let Christine know that they could, 'smell burning.' That woman has the patience of a saint as I am categorically telling you now that my responses would not have been classed as 'cheeky.'

And predictably, the electrician didn't have the part to mend the fridge the next day, so our sales of cooked meats took a real hit. It's the old adage, 'If they can't see it, they can't buy it.'

It took three more days for the spark to show his face. We discovered, via the village grapevine of course, that he did have the essential fridge part, but had decided to prioritise a more lucrative job. My wife, frustrated by the financial void of selling no sliced beef that week, gave him an earbashing that would make any man rue the day he was born.

Chapter 17   Family Matters

Though our eldest (aka number one) had fled the nest years before, we were still busy rearing numbers two and three alongside everything else. The pressure of opening a shop at 8.30am, knowing customers would be pacing and tutting if we were a second late, together with ensuring two hormone crazed daughters hauled their carcasses out of bed, carried out ablutions to a standard that would not provoke a referral to social services, and were dropped off at a school which was a fair few miles away, was, without doubt, a major achievement in our daily lives.

When number two acquired a boyfriend, we named him, "The Door" as he did nothing but hang around.

We were never going to make a decent living with these kids in tow. Their addiction to dousing their Sunday lunches with mint sauce would wipe out our annual profit margin on condiments in one sitting.

Chapter 18   Multitasking

Whilst some days the trade was worryingly slow, we had plenty of days where we were rushed off our feet. I recall one morning when six customers came into the shop at the same time and began jostling each other to decide who would be served first. In the midst of such mayhem, a lorry load of sand arrived for my next building job. The driver asking me, "Where should I put it?" had me biting my lip to stop me replying with you know what. Things only got worse when in waltzed Hilda, who loved nothing more than a busy shop, not only for the banter, but she used the additional bodies as a smoke screen to hide her inability to count correctly. Whenever she picked up six pies and then whisked them into a paper bag with a sleight of hand that even the lovely Debbie McGee would marvel at, she would always confidently declare, "There are three pies in there." Of course, we knew all her little tricks; revenge would be ours by overcharging her for fruit, veg and meat that we weighed on the scales. The village rumour mill regularly reported that Hilda's husband was unwilling (and unable) to fulfil her other marital requirements – he'd never get away with it now thanks to the invention of Viagra.

Chapter 19 Hull's Bells

Despite the early start and long drive, I never tired of our visits to the warehouse in Hull to buy our stocks. As part of the process of paying for our purchases at the checkout, we had to give proof of our status as private business owners. The young man at the till checked our paperwork and asked, "Where's Tibthorpe?" "Two miles from Wetwang," I replied, "It's a place with trees, grass, flowers and peace and quiet.

His two remaining teeth miraculously appeared in what must have been his best customer service smile. "Where's that then," he replied. "Are you a carrot cruncher?" This type of interaction is like bread and butter to me.

"Is it true that Hitler bombed the shit out of Hull and only did four quid's worth of damage then?" I asked. His response, "Who's Hitler?," told me everything I already knew about this resident of the aforementioned Kingstown. Obviously, this young man was not shaping up to be an influential member of the team bidding for Hull to host 'European City of Culture,' years later.

On yet another visit to the warehouse in Hull, we were met with cashiers sporting red baseball caps emblazoned with the Coca Cola logo. "I feel like a right dick head with this 'at' on," moaned one young lad. "It's Mr Wong's fault. He's making us do this," replied his fellow till op. What else could I say other than, "Two Wongs don't make it right lads." The retort, "Bollocks to you, carrot muncher," was well deserved on this occasion.. The red caps were still being worn by the staff months later. Rumour had it that they'd started up a dance troupe called the 'Red Hot Boys.'

Chapter 20   The Shopkeeper's Nark

Every Thursday, regular as clockwork, we would receive a delivery from Prime Pak Meats. Their delivery man was clearly not commission based as he was never pushy and seemed in no rush to move on to his next deliver. He was always eager to tell us exactly what other village shops were selling and at what price. We prided ourselves on only selling products that were 100% meat. Particularly when the nark divulged that all the supermarkets want meat pumped with water so they can sell it cheap.

Chapter 21 On tick

We'd had a particularly busy day, but when we cashed up that night, the till seemed relatively empty. "There's more tick than a clock in here," I sighed. "The buggers can't get tick in Tesco," replied Christine despondently. "Not yet anyway."

Chapter 21 Tricks of the trade

When customers came in asking for boxes of chocolates – usually just before Mother's day or Christmas, we would always pick up our most expensive and our least expensive boxes and hold them in front of the customer. It really didn't matter to us if they picked the most expensive or the cheapest; our profit margin was the same on both boxes, but they always chose one of the boxes, one hundred percent of the time.

We were always mad busy before bank holidays. Obviously, we weren't complaining as the money was rolling in. What was torturous about the whole thing though was getting the bread order right. The indignation people showed if they couldn't buy their daily loaf was tangible. Yet too much ordered meant that number 2 and number 3 would be eating toast with everything for weeks on end afterwards. The same went for cold meats, dairy products and any other product that had gone past its sell by date. Whatever we couldn't sell in time, we had to concoct a meal from to serve to our perpetually starving hungry daughters (or 'pick up bailers' as I used to refer to them).

There had been an unrelenting north easterly wind for days which howled through the shop and sent newspapers flying everywhere every time a customer opened the door. Even the most highly coiffed customers were walking in with hair like Ken Dodd, and every single one of them moaned about the weather. Always the salesman, I suggested that they might want to look at our selection of woolly hats on sale. We shifted loads. Good old British weather.

Chapter 22 The mystery of the blemished underpants

Another onerous role placed upon us appeared to be taking responsibility for lost and found items in the vicinity. Jean Marsden strode into the shop one afternoon and announced to all, "Somebody has thrown a pair of men's underpants into the hedge on Pump Lane and they are covered in 'bab.' Little Eric, also in the shop at the time, in his broad Yorkshire accent asked loudly, "Where they really larded up wi' shit?" No-one could ever claim that Yorkshire men are pretentious.

Later that evening at 6.15pm the phone rang. "Hello chap. Can I have a twelve-inch pizza, chap? I'll start walking to the shop." Do I even need to say that it was a Saturday?

Chap stumbled into the shop a few minutes later and I took the opportunity to ask him if he'd lost a pair of underpants that were covered in bab. "I don't think so chap, but I will check," he slurred. He promptly pulled down his trousers and began to examine the contents of his underpants – his 'three piece suite' on full show. Delighted that the underpants in question did not belong to him, he pulled his trousers back up and left the shop with his pizza. Both Christine and I burst out laughing and we both agreed that he wouldn't remember anything about this in the morning.

Christine spent the next day asking the customers if they had lost a pair of underpants. Little Eric, who lived down the now notorious Pump Lane, came into the shop in the late afternoon and told us that, "There were folk stopping by to look at them all day long."

The mystery continued into the next day with customers still debating about the possible owner. No one was safe from suspicion – Our lady PC came into the shop and announced to all had been off work all week with the 'shits', blaming a bad curry she had consumed in a local pub. I asked her if she wore men's underpants. "No I bloody don't, but I saw the underpants down Pump Lane." To ease the false accusation, I told her that it was a shame that our promotional offer of 2 for 1 rolls of toilet paper had ended last week. Juliet Bravo made a hasty retreat, hissing, "Very funny, Jerry. If I didn't have to go to the toilet right now, I would bloody hit you."

Chapter 23 – Days off

Our days off were few and far between as we really did 'open all hours' whenever we could. We travelled to a food trade show in Willerby where everything was marked as 30% off. As far as I'm concerned, if they can afford to knock 30% off the price, then the price is 30% too expensive in the first place. Later that day we travelled over to meet our friend and fellow shopkeeper of the only village shop in Dalton in the Wolds. We all ranted for two and a half hours about how much we hated owning a shop and we left despondent, feeling like we were driving back to our very own prison.

But there were many good days when the customers were appreciative and got their hands in their pockets. Mainly those when the sun was shining, and choc ices were selling like hot cakes.

After yet another supermarket sweep at the warehouse, we decided to pay a visit to see my mate Dikko in Middleton in the Wolds. He's one of those blokes who always tries to sell you something. As we were driving home with his and hers matching wrist watches, and a Sky satellite dish, I said to Christine, "We must be bloody nuts." She replied, "We are bloody nuts to own a shop."

Months later, we called in again to see Dikko. We'd both had 'the talk' as we were driving there that we wouldn't buy anything this time, no matter what he offered us. The bike we bought for forty pounds fitted snugly into the back of the van. I swear to God, if Dikko ever opened a shop near ours, our business would be doomed with his ability to sell sand to the Arabs.

After a particularly busy Saturday, Christine and I set off to Beverley to buy some videos to sell in the shop. On our return, we immediately noticed that a motorbike had pulled up directly behind our van. I saw a man with a hammer smash the back window of the van. He heard me shouting and sped off on his bike.

Despite us reporting the crime immediately at Beverley Police station, we were told that there was nothing they could do as we couldn't tell them the vehicle registration number on his motorbike. What I will say is that I got a bloody good look at him, and one day, I will see the bastard. Every dog has his day.

The number of times I looked at Christine and she was absolutely knackered from these long hours in the shop. I knew she needed a holiday, but a) we couldn't afford one and b) we couldn't afford to close the shop. That is until our friends in Scotland contacted us and invited us to stay with them for three days in May. As an annual holiday, that wouldn't suffice for most. But for shopkeepers, one day's holiday is like a week for your average punter.

One of my diary entries reads, 'On our way back from the warehouse, Christine and I went into Beverley. She to have her hair done (£17), me to have my feet done (£8). I have no idea why I felt it relevant to write the cost down. It was obviously an exciting prospect to escape 'the prison' and having my corns removed was preferable to being in the shop.

Chapter 24 Village sweepstakes

Sweepstakes provided us all with a little bit of excitement and we organised many throughout our time at the shop. The most popular was always the Grand National. On this, and every other big sporting occasion, the shop would always be jampacked before and after the event, but never during. This suited us as we could hang up our aprons and watch whatever was happening in our front room.

One particular April, we were extremely peeved when we heard the shop doorbell ring mid-way through the Grand National which we both avidly watching. When Christine walked into the shop, Helena was waiting for her to be served and remarked upon the lack of customers. "The Grand National is on now," Christine barked at her. "I don't bloody care about horses," Helena replied.

When Christine came back into the front room, the race was over and she was suitably annoyed. She recounted Helena's words and added. "If the jockeys were riding naked, she wouldn't have come into the shop.

Harry Brookes won £17.50 in the Grand National sweepstake that year. That was a decent amount back then.

Chapter 25 Local politics

The crazy world of politics had little relevance in our life as shopkeepers. That was until Driffield Council decided to hike up the rates for local shopkeepers. To register my disdain of this move, I decided that I would attend a meeting in Driffield one spring evening to discuss my personal concerns about this plan. Predictably it was a complete waste of my time and the room was full of hot air. The local Tory MP had, presumably under duress, agreed to deign us with his unworthy presence. He said bugger all and just kept looking at his watch and taking his glasses on and off with a delusional air of self- importance. As I left, I said to a fellow shopkeeper, "Waste of petrol coming here tonight. I should have stayed at home and finished painting me kitchen ceiling."

Chapter 26 Sick pay

When I raised a pint in the Royal standard to being self-employed all those years ago, what I'd failed to acknowledge was that sick pay was no longer a 'thing.' If I didn't work, the repercussions were huge. Quite simply, I couldn't earn money to feed my family or pay my bills or mortgage. So, over many years, I literally dragged myself into work in all weathers, and did the best I could, despite flu, broken bones and every other debilitating ailment that life can throw at you.

This sick day was on another level. I woke up with the most excruciatingly painful headache I'd ever known (and before the thought even crosses your mind, it absolutely was not alcohol induced).

I could not lift my head off the pillow, and the stars in my eyes were definitely not channelling Matthew

Kelly. At 9am, I took two tablets. Time passed in a blur and I swallowed two more. Sometime later, the headache was still raging, so I necked a couple more. This pattern continued over a period of time that, at this stage, I was no longer coherent enough to quantify. I woke up at 2 o'clock in the afternoon- a different man.

Full of beans and thrilled to be headache free, I bounced into the shop and informed Christine that I was fit for work again. I'm not bloody surprised. In just six hours of delirium, I had unwittingly imbibed 15 co-codamols. Christine did her nut when I told her. However, if you've ever suffered from a crucifying migraine, you will do anything it takes to rid yourself of the pain.

Chapter 27 – Village Leaks

Helena was acting strangely. She must have put a packet of hobnobs in, then out of her basket at least eight times. She glanced over at me repeatedly to the extent that I felt extremely uncomfortable. I heard her hiss, "Christine I need to talk to you." I sensed a discussion about 'woman's troubles,' so I fled the shop like a rat up a drainpipe.

I had barely left the room when Helena divulged to Christine that she had been to the Doctor's about her weak bladder – apparently her mother had also suffered with the same condition. My wife, not known for her tact and diplomacy, asked Helena if she peed herself. "All the time, Christine, "confessed the poor woman. "It's really getting me down."

She began to describe a contraption that her Doctor had given her to help with this medical embarrassment. "He's given me this rubber thing that you plug in and it vibrates around your tummy."

At this point, Christine burst into laughter, joined by Helena who, despite her ailment, was able to see the funny side of what she had just said. I heard them laughing hysterically for three solid minutes, until Christine shouted out, "Oh God I've wet myself." In between laughs and gulping for air, Helena shouted, "Go and get your own vibrating belt. You're not having mine."

Prologue

Thirty years later, I can look back on our venture into the world of retail with some fondness and happy memories of the good times we shared. My wife and I are now very happily retired in a beautiful part of the Lake District and enjoying the peace and beauty all around us. Every time we drive past a remote village shop, our hearts go out to the hardworking staff who are inside – freezing cold, no doubt, and worried sick about how they can scratch a living from such a thankless job.

Printed in Great Britain
by Amazon

18734122R00041